THE POLAR BEAR

BY LISA OWINGS

BELLWETHER MEDIA • MINNEAPOLIS, MN

This edition first published in 2013 by Bellwether Media, Inc.

No part of this publication may be reproduced in whole or in part without written permission of the publisher. For information regarding permission, write to Bellwether Media, Inc., Attention: Permissions Department, 5357 Penn Avenue South, Minneapolis, MN 55419.

Library of Congress Cataloging-in-Publication Data

Owings, Lisa.
 The polar bear / by Lisa Owings.
   pages cm. – (Pilot. Nature's deadliest)
 Includes bibliographical references and index.
 Summary: "Fascinating images accompany information about the polar bear. The combination of high-interest subject matter and narrative text is intended for students in grades 3 through 7"–Provided by publisher.
 Audience: Ages 8-12.
 ISBN 978-1-60014-882-8 (hardcover : alk. paper)
 1. Polar bear–Juvenile literature. 2. Bear attacks–Juvenile literature. I. Title.
 QL737.C27O974 2013
 599.784–dc23
                                            2012041219

Printed in the United States of America, North Mankato, MN.

CONTENTS

Terror in the Arctic

It was about 10:30 p.m. in northern Canada. The summer sun was still high in the sky. Alice Annanack decided she wanted to go for a walk. She peered out the windows of the cabin where she was staying with her husband, Tommy. They never went outside without checking for polar bears. The coast seemed to be clear. Alice stepped out into the brightly lit night.

Suddenly, Alice heard a noise. She thought it was her husband. Instead, she turned to see the face of an angry polar bear. It was only two steps away. Alice stood frozen in terror as the bear **lunged** toward her. Then its powerful jaws closed around her skull. Alice's screams echoed across the campground.

Polar Bears in the Wild

Between 20,000 and 25,000 polar bears currently live in the wild. As many as 15,000 of them live in Canada.

Alice felt her scalp tearing away. The polar bear's teeth drilled into her skull. They were close to piercing her brain. But Alice would not give up without a fight. She brought a hand up to shield her head. The bear crushed her **fragile** limb in its jaws. Then it continued to **maul** her head. Pain flooded her body. Still Alice fought.

Tommy heard his wife's screams. He rushed outside with a rifle and aimed for the bear's hind legs. He pulled the trigger. Nothing happened. Tommy raced back inside for his other gun. Alice felt the bear's claws rip into her back. Then the animal began dragging her away. Alice did not lose hope. *I refuse to be killed by you*, she thought.

Close Calls

The bear's teeth were just 0.08 inches (2 millimeters) away from Alice's brain. Its claws came within 0.4 inches (1 centimeter) of her spine.

Alice was still fighting for her life when Tommy returned.
He fired a shot at the beast's hind legs. The bear let go
of Alice. Tommy finally had a clear shot at its head. He took it.
The polar bear died instantly.

Tommy knew he had to act fast to save his wife. He carried
Alice into the cabin. He bandaged her wounds with rags and
radioed for help. No one answered. Alice would have to hold
on until morning.

Tommy would not let his wife sleep. He feared she would not wake up. After hours of suffering, help arrived. Alice was flown to a Montreal hospital for emergency surgery. She would have a long recovery. But she had survived a polar bear attack!

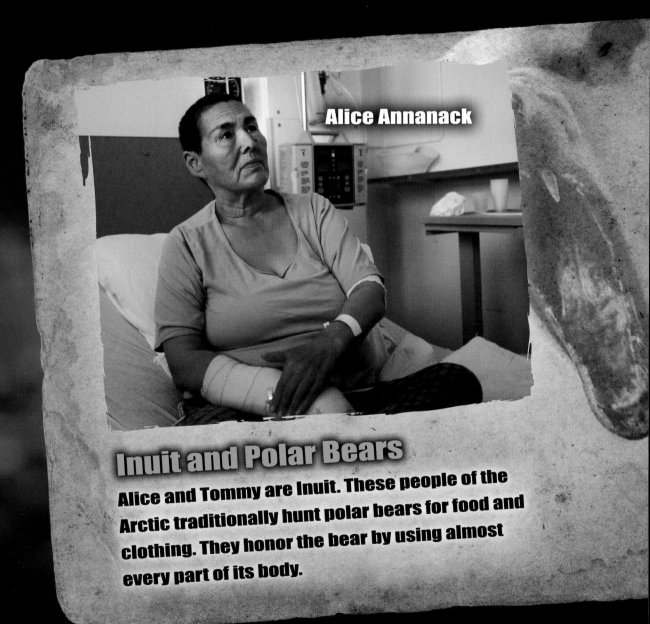

Alice Annanack

Inuit and Polar Bears

Alice and Tommy are Inuit. These people of the Arctic traditionally hunt polar bears for food and clothing. They honor the bear by using almost every part of its body.

A Cold Killer

The polar bear is one of the largest and deadliest predators on Earth. It has no fear of other animals or humans. The bear is built to survive in the harsh Arctic environment. White fur helps it hide against snow and ice. A thick layer of fat keeps it warm.

A male polar bear can pack on more than 1,600 pounds (725 kilograms). Large paws up to 1 foot (0.3 meters) wide support and spread out the polar bear's weight. This lets the bear stalk prey on thin ice. Pads on the paws prevent slipping. Sharp, curved claws help the bear rip apart flesh.

polar bear   human

polar bear territory = ▭

N
W E
S

Super Swimmers

Polar bears have webbing between their toes to help them paddle through water. They can swim more than 100 miles (160 kilometers) without stopping to rest!

Seals are a polar bear's favorite food. Polar bears hunt them in a few different ways. One method is to find a hole in the ice where seals come up to breathe. A polar bear waits silently for hours for a seal to surface. The bear **strikes** the instant one does. It clamps its jaws over the seal's head and crushes its skull. Then it hauls its feast from the water.

Another method is to sneak up on a sunbathing seal. Polar bears can smell a seal from as many as 20 miles (32 kilometers) away. The bear creeps slowly toward its **unsuspecting** prey. It stays silent and low to the ground until it gets close. Then the bear **charges**. The seal is ripped apart in a flash of teeth and claws.

Easy Prey

Sometimes a polar bear smells baby seals in a den beneath the snow. The hungry bear crushes the roof of the den with its giant paws. It digs the seals out and eats them.

Male polar bears become **aggressive** toward one another during the mating season. Their fighting begins as playful practice. Later, the fights become serious. The bears stand to their full height of 8 feet (2.5 meters) or more. They show their teeth and bite at their rival's face and neck. They slash at each other with their claws. Sometimes polar bears fight to the death.

Mothers and Cubs

A female polar bear eats and eats before she settles into her winter den. This food keeps her alive until spring. It also helps her nourish the cubs she gives birth to in the den.

Male polar bears sometimes kill and eat cubs. Female polar bears will do anything to protect their young. They will even challenge male bears twice their size. Female bears also fight males for food when hunting is poor. Polar bear mothers must feed their cubs!

Polar Bear Attacks

A hungry polar bear is one of the most dangerous animals to humans. Most other kinds of bears attack people only in defense. However, polar bears have been known to attack people for food. The best way to avoid an attack is to stay away from polar bear territory. Polar bears normally live and hunt within 100 miles (160 kilometers) of the Arctic coast.

If you choose to enter polar bear territory, keep watch for bears at all times. It is safest to travel in daylight with a large group. Pack any food in sealed containers. Carry **bear spray** with you in case of an attack. If you see a bear, back away slowly. If the bear notices you, speak to it calmly. The bear should recognize that you are not its usual prey.

See the Signs

Watch for these signs that a polar bear may be nearby:

- large paw prints
- droppings
- fresh kills, especially dead seals
- claw marks or freshly dug holes

If the polar bear sees you as a threat, continue backing away slowly. Any fast or aggressive movement can anger the bear. Avoid making eye contact. If the polar bear is stalking you, make loud noises. Try to look large and threatening. Stay close to the group you are traveling with.

Never run from a polar bear. Instead, get your bear spray ready. Spray the bear if it charges to within 30 feet (9 meters) of you. Prepare to fight if the bear keeps coming. Use anything you have with you to stab its nose or eyes. Protect your head and neck if you can. Remember that you are fighting for your life!

Angry Bear

If a polar bear sees you as a threat, it might...

- growl
- pant
- hiss
- snap its jaws
- stomp its feet
- stare directly at you
- lower its head
- flatten its ears

polar bears, it is easy to see they are special. They thrive in a place where most other life would not survive. Sadly, many experts believe polar bears will be nearing **extinction** within the next hundred years. Earth is slowly warming. This **climate change** is melting the ice where polar bears hunt. It is getting harder and harder for them to find food.

We can help polar bears by learning more about them. It is also important to learn about climate change. People can help slow climate change by using less energy. That means doing things like making less waste and traveling by bike instead of by car. We can each do our part to make sure these mighty bears walk the earth for centuries to come.

aggressive—violent or threatening

bear spray—a kind of pepper spray for bears; it can stop a bear from attacking by causing a burning sensation in the eyes.

charges—rushes forward to attack

climate change—the gradual warming of Earth and other changes in weather

extinction—the process of disappearing from the Earth

fragile—easily broken

lunged—leaped forward suddenly

maul—to injure with deep wounds

strikes—attacks suddenly and forcefully

unsuspecting—not aware of a possible danger

To Learn More

At the Library

Olson, Gillia M. *Polar Bears' Search for Ice: A Cause and Effect Investigation*. Mankato, Minn.: Capstone Press, 2011.

Rosing, Norbert. *Polar Bears*. Richmond Hill, Ont.: Firefly Books, 2010.

Taylor, Barbara. *Arctic & Antarctic*. New York, N.Y.: DK Pub., 2012.

On the Web

Learning more about polar bears is as easy as 1, 2, 3.

1. Go to www.factsurfer.com.

2. Enter "polar bears" into the search box.

3. Click the "Surf" button and you will see a list of related Web sites.

With factsurfer.com, finding more information is just a click away.

Index